LOST AVENUES

Nick Fletcher is an award-winning writer whose work has appeared in many UK magazines and newspapers. He is also the author of two crime novels, two short story collections and three books on antiques and collecting. This is his second book of poetry.

His poetry has appeared in the Poetry Today anthologies Footprints In Time and De Facto, and in the national women's magazine Company.

Nick Fletcher lives in South Devon where he works as a freelance writer.

GH00597997

Also by Nick Fletcher

Novels

The Long Sunset
Imperfect Day

Short Story Collections

Escaping the Rain
Snapshot

Poetry

Dark Heart

Lost Avenues

Love Poems

NICK FLETCHER

Classic Books

First published in 2016
by Classic Books
TQ5 0HG

Printed in Great Britain by TJ International Ltd
Padstow, Cornwall

British Library Cataloguing in Publication Data.
A catalogue record for this book is available
from the British Library.

ISBN 978 - 0 - 9519399 - 9 - 4

Editorial consultant:
Eve Kerswill

Contents

Author's Note

For many people, love – or the search for it – can be the driving force of life. Some believe that somewhere, there is just one special person for them, someone who can fulfil their dreams and desires. Others take a more logical view, that given the billions of people on the planet, there are – statistically at least – many potential partners capable of being their true love. However, as they are scattered across the globe, we are unlikely to find them all. So we should count ourselves lucky if we discover just one.

These poems touch on many aspects of love: finding it, handling it, and sometimes losing it. Being in love is a unique emotional experience which can define us, enhance us and underpin the purpose of life itself.

Love is a constant. It remains at the core of the human condition. If we are fortunate enough to find true love, we should try to hold on to it. It may be our only opportunity.

Nick Fletcher
South Devon, England

Catching The Breeze

I don't suppose
you recall that day,
the country walk,
bleak hill top
almost colourless
in midwinter.
Or our laughter
as we tried to catch
the tugging
blustery breeze,
hands outstretched,
clutching at the
cold racing air.
Being together
was still new and
achingly important,
full of promise
yet edged with
faint uncertainty.
Nothing much
happened that day,
except catching the breeze.
I don't know where
you are now
but I want you to know
I can still catch the breeze.
I'm holding it,
letting it scent my touch
before I release it,
watch it soar high
across the hills
on its way
to find you.

Love Me

Love me
as if it's September,
with its warmth and its glow
and its gold.
Love me
in past and in present.
Love me
when I am old.
Love me
with passion and longing.
Love me
with cries in the night.
Love me
for no other reason
than to you my wrongs
still seem right.
Love me
as if I am perfect.
Love me
unfettered and free.
Love me
as if it's September.
That's how I want love to be.

A Thousand Stars

I stare at the night sky,
watching
a thousand stars
in just the tiny
portion of space
within my gaze.
You are not here
to see them
but by email
we have arranged
for you to look up
at this precise time.
I want you to see
those thousand stars
against the backdrop
of billions more,
and see each one
as an eternal
silver spark
of my love for you.

Apology In A Darkened Room

Sharp shafts of sunlight
from the shuttered windows
split the darkness into narrow fans
and I pause for a few seconds
to allow my eyes to adjust.
Then I see you in the doorway,
leaning casually on the frame,
looking at me directly,
your face a mask of non-expression.
I didn't expect you to be there.
Our quarrel had been raw
and deeply wounding,
your walk-out expected
and probably terminal.
Now, you see my hesitation
and step forward,
standing close enough
to put a cool finger on my lips.
'Don't say anything,'
you tell me with oiled softness.
In a smooth deft movement
you begin to unbutton my shirt.
You never did apologise
in a formal way.
That was one of the things
about you that I loved.

Blue

Looking south
there is the sea,
alluring distant blue
beneath exquisite sky,
pale flinty blue
and cloudless.
Such beauty
overpowers,
holds me to the spot,
my thoughts restrained,
my eyes addicted.
Then there you are,
smiling blue eyes,
simple white shirt,
faded blue jeans,
sun on your hair.
And I dismiss
the sea and sky.

Dash In The Rain

I hate the rain.
It seems to have been
raining for weeks.
We stand hesitantly
under the cafe awning
waiting for the moment
to sprint to the car.
But the hard, spiteful rain
doesn't want to ease
so we have to brave it.
We run hand in hand,
me with head down,
you shrieking with
shock and delight.
We fall into the car,
laughing and cursing
and shaking our heads
like big wet dogs.
You peel off your top
and start to wring it out,
stray rivulets glistening
on your naked breasts.
I take off my own
sodden shirt
and use it to pat you dry.
I love the rain.

Bright Light

When I look
into your eyes
I do not see
deep blue pools
with hidden depths,
nor Cicero's
mirrors of the soul.
I see only honesty
and innocence
and even after
all this time
undiminished love
shining out
like the bright
unsullied light
of the rising sun.

Thoughts

You send me
healing thoughts,
flashing and gliding
across the miles
like sleek birds,
riding the currents,
seeking me out,
flurrying around me
wafting warmth
and comfort
and all the love
of a lifetime.

Invitation

Music drifts up
from the busy bar
four floors below
the apartment,
a soothing balm
on the nagging ache
of being alone.
I asked you to come,
told you Barcelona
would still be hot
in early October,
described the sea view,
the narrow lanes
infused with tiny shops
and cool cafes,
the street market
and book shops.
You refused
my invitation
in your usual way,
feigning indifference
and saying nothing.
Perhaps this time
I should have asked you
out loud.

Intent

Early evening, late November,
first visit to your apartment,
just far enough away
from Western Avenue
for the drone of traffic
to be hushed.
The living room has large
framed landscape paintings,
each individually lit
and appearing to be windows
to a less troubled world.
You are wearing
a vermilion dress
and you wear it
exactly as such a dress
should be worn.
A champagne bottle juts
from the frosted ice bucket
and two tall glasses
stand on a scattering
of crushed rose petals.
Your intent
is unmistakable.
I am looking forward
to our first-year anniversary.
Because tonight marks
just our first week.

The Fate Of Glass

A proverb says
the fate of glass
is to break.
On dark days
I ponder
whether I too
am destined
to be broken
by my expectation
of true love,
how much of it
you can give,
and for how long.
Perhaps my fate
is not to break,
just to wait.

Imagination

I lie very quietly
in the afternoon sun,
wind chimes tinkling
random tunes,
geraniums and marigolds
a nodding chorus line.
I imagine you here,
stretched out
on the next sunbed,
languid in the heat,
perhaps asleep
behind those big
sunglasses.
I would reach across,
entwine fingers,
study the texture
of your taut tanned skin,
murmur inaudibly
things I can't say
to you out loud.
Imagination
brings us close
but not close enough.
I miss the cool
charged frisson
of your touch.

Gone

First time I saw you
I should have been
less reticent.
That word and others
are too small,
too inadequate
to explain or justify
my frozen stance.
I was reticent
for too long,
spoke with dullness
and distant hope.
Always struggling
to find the right words,
by the time I found
the honed phrases
and the confidence
you had gone.

Forgotten Dance

You say that a long time ago,
we danced.
My recollection is eroded
to the fine dust
of a crowded life
but I like to think
that on that night
I held you close
as we slowly circled,
and whispered
that I loved you.
But it wasn't like that.
I would have been too
awkward, too scared
of being rejected
to say the words
I longed to say.
So we just danced.
And life danced on,
spinning us away
in different directions.

Details

I recall many details
of that secret day.
The silver pendant,
the unreal blue
of your eyes,
the dandelion tea,
political discussion,
the waiter's surprise
when I order sausages
for your dog,
dutifully curled up
by the table.
And later, of course,
that parking ticket.
Yet my lingering,
most vivid memory
is the long entwined hug,
and me gently kissing
the tip of your nose

Code

Late July evening,
watching the sunset
while I wait.
Maybe you will come,
though two times
out of three
you don't.
Don't is the wrong word.
It implies you have a choice.
Can't is more accurate,
because you can't
often get away.
I imagine your arrival,
flustered and a little anxious.
You never say hello,
just merge into my arms,
kissing and holding tight.
Then, a stolen hour
of moments I will reprise
on my dying day.
I lean against the car door
watching dark clouds
closing down the sky
against the sliding sun.
Through a small gap
bright orange light
bursts through,
the beam a pathway
to the heavens,
or perhaps for me
a gateway to hell.
A breeze chills the air,
and the cooling
car exhaust cracks
like Morse code.
Seven cracks,
seven letters.
I don't know Morse code
but I think they spell
You Fool.

Back To You

It was dark when I set off
and I never glanced back.
When I came to crossroads
I destroyed the signposts.
Bridges burned and collapsed
behind me as I travelled on,
and I scrubbed out my tracks
in the mud and snow.
The route was obliterated,
a ghost trail in a foggy haze,
invisible, never again to be found.
Yet at the end of my journey
I find myself
right back at the start,
tapping at your door
like a timid child.

Coming Close

There were several
who came close,
lingered on for weeks
or even months.
All had a certain look,
tousled blonde hair,
shy teasing eyes.
Some felt it would work,
had dreamy hopes,
whispered, sighed,
fulfilled desires.
Yet when I failed
to love them,
their icy eyes
demanded reasons.
I couldn't tell them
it was because
none of them
was you.

Clear Mind

I have cleared my mind
of all irrelevant matters.
All surplus information
has been erased,
self-doubt discarded,
hopes and ambition
callously banished,
memories and dreams
unrepentantly deleted,
a lifelime of knowledge
ruthlessly removed.
All that remains now
is the core of my life,
my reason to exist.
Pure and undiluted,
my love for you.

You Know Me

You know all I am
and all I am not
and there is more
of the latter.
Yet you took me back
without my ever
going away.
It just seemed
as if I had.
Knowing who I am
and what I am
and loving both
gives you ownership.
I am yours.
Unprotestingly.

Watching

I lie very still
and silent,
alert for any detail,
any clue
that may signal
its appearance.
No spy
has carried out
surveillance
with greater care
and diligence,
no keener sense
of anticipation.
I watch
second by second,
minute my minute
until it happens.
Sometimes,
you smile
in your sleep.

The Lighthouse

I kiss you by the lighthouse
as its beam divides the night
and the darkness folds around us
and the stars begin their flight.
They swoop down
and fly around us
like tiny silver birds
ready to be witnesses,
to hear me say the words.
I tell you that I love you,
my love is steeled and pure,
that the sky and earth could vanish
but my love would still endure.
On the cliff at Berry Head
the lighthouse brands its name,
but now its flash is rivalled
by our enduring flame.

True

When you told me
you would always
be truthful
unless it was
essential to lie,
that in itself was
total honesty.
Yet it made you
no easier to assess,
to understand,
or to believe,
particularly
on that warm
starlit night
when you
told me
you loved me.

Who We Are

It's not important
that we know
who we are.
Life has shaped us,
so too love
and sometimes
lack of it.
Past lives leave
indelible stains
and scars on
our fragile
emotional facade.
Who we are now
may be someone
we want to change,
but cannot.
What is important
is that we remember
who we once were.

Twelve Minutes

Heavy stifling
July evening.
The air has a tired,
downbeat feel
and even the drone
of passing traffic
seems lethargic.
I'm on the terrace
at Rafini's and you
are twelve minutes late.
Then I see you
coming up the steps,
bright eyes and
careless smile.
When you get to
my table,
you don't say hello,
just lean down
and briefly kiss me
on the cheek.
You sit down,
flick back your hair
and ask me to order
sparkling water
with two slices of lime.
You add please
in your soft
drawn-out tone.
Twelve minutes late.
Could have been twelve years.
I'd have still waited.

The Company Of Ghosts

We stood in the cathedral crypt:
chilled air, half-dark
and a thousand years
of silent stoic stone.
You said you saw the ghosts
of lives and loves long past,
but you were not afraid.
I wanted to kiss you
but it was not the right place,
though it offered seclusion,
a lover's sanctuary.
So we kissed.
Above us, visitors walked quietly
admiring the serene beauty
of the sunlit stained glass,
but we preferred
the company of ghosts
to share the moment.
I didn't think the ghosts
would mind us kissing.
Nor God.
There is no wrong place for love.

The One

Lazing on the terrace,
in late diluted sun,
reading Leonard Cohen
because he is The One.
He has witnessed
all of love,
the power, the passion
and the blood.
He scalpels love,
he pares it thin,
exposes why
we seldom win.
His view of love
is worldly,
his wisdom
clear to see,
and he says that
True Love Leaves No Trace
yet I must disagree.
Love puts its imprint on us,
its DNA is strong.
True love brands us
heart and soul.
Cohen must be wrong.

Best Day

The best day with you
was not when snowfall
kept us marooned
the whole weekend,
lazing by the fire
sipping mulled wine
and whispering promises.
The best day with you
was not at the Spanish villa
when you danced naked
in the moonlight
around the swimming pool.
The best day with you
was not even the time
you first murmured
I love you
as we kissed in the rain.
The best day with you
isn't a memory,
not a place,
not a moment,
not a dream.
Best day with you
is tomorrow.

The Call

My mobile phone is placed
like a compass pointing
to the strongest signal.
It has been so long.
Decades have drifted by
since the last words,
the final kiss.
Now, we are sure to be
different people:
reshaped, redefined,
maybe diminished
by passing time.
Yet after an email exchange
you said you would call.
The phone rings.
Patchy connection.
You sound far away,
hesitant and nervous
and I blurt out
too much, too soon.
I keep talking,
trying but failing
not to dwell
on the time
when we were nineteen
and uncertain
where life would take us.
Doesn't really matter
why it didn't work,
though youth and ambition
would stand accused.
During the call
tones soften,
and curiosity
establishes itself.
Still a little uncertain,
you agree we should meet.
For the first time today,
I stop shaking.

The Beach

The sea trudges in,
flat, dark and oily,
looking old and tired
and barely able
to flop onto the beach.
You said you wouldn't come
and I knew you meant it
but I turned up anyway,
my hope so small
it could cower
beneath a dust speck.
It's late in the day
and low daubed clouds
nuzzle each other,
plotting their next move
with faint menace.
I stand on the tide line
in uneasy surreal
grey light,
alone with a broken day.
Not quite alone.
On the rocks I see
two Sabine gulls
moodily circling each other,
pecking and shrieking.
I almost envy them.

Smudges

Somehow, it seems
we are being watched
though logic would tell us
this is not the case.
We are just two people
kissing by a parked car,
smudges
against a drab
urban background,
unidentifiable
blurred images
like those created
by Monet.
Fused by our kiss
we create
for just moments
our own unsigned
Impressionist painting.

Symmetry

Face down on a lounger,
you seemed asleep
but your feet tapped
the air to music
from your iPod.
I knelt alongside,
kissing your shoulder.
The smell and taste
of soft hot flesh
encouraged me
to string kisses
all the way down
your spine,
veering off to place
the final kiss
on the left cheek
of your bottom.
You giggled and asked me
to get you a cold drink.
I leaned forward
and kissed the right cheek.
I have always been
a slave to symmetry.

Silent Sunday Morning

Nothing is quite as silent
as Sunday morning.
Everyday sounds are
excluded or diminished.
Traffic drone fades,
barking dogs slumber,
phones lie mute and useless.
I turn over and listen
to your soft easy breathing,
watch the gentle movement
of your breasts
above the sheet.
I want to kiss them
but it is too early.
There should be
no movement, no noise
to breach the sanctuary.
Not just yet.
The day is still unfolding.
Nothing is as silent
as Sunday morning.

Should Have Known

The rain has set in,
falling hard,
scrabbling at the window,
seeking me out,
trying to wash away
the stain of regret.
Hot caressing sun
on the stucco walls
of the Marbella villa
and our long days
of bed and wine
and little else
have all retreated
to the awkward
outer edges of memory.
At the end of
that long summer
you left,
troubled by uncertainty
and infuriating indecision.
You should have stayed,
noticed the nuances
and tender touches.
Now autumn has closed in,
belligerent
and unforgiving.
Incessant rain
erodes my spirit.
Our kind of love
comes just once.
But only I knew that.

Shadow

I stand by the window,
early morning sun
harshly bright.
The light gives strength,
lasers the scars,
cleanses the spirit,
leaves me at ease.
Dazzling light,
new day fresh,
pure and forceful
protects me
from the whiplash
of memory.
But only for a moment.
Then I see your shadow
intently edging in.

Replay

Our past moves away,
the pace slow
but relentless,
dragging with it
our memories.
We try to cling to those
which matter most,
for comfort,
sentiment,
to re-touch
the emotions.
Some memories slip
through the tiny fissures
in a fading mind.
If that process begins,
if memories slide away
unseen, unheard
into the outer darkness,
I want just one to remain,
etched forever
for endless replay.
You.

Promises

It was one of those summers
which made many promises
and mostly kept them,
gifting eternal sunshine,
perfect riverside picnics,
late-night drives
and eventually
a detailed exploration
of the contortional limits
of a two-seater car.
After, we flipped back the hood
and stared at a high moon
and said the right words
for then
but not for later.
We were captured
by the moment,
entranced
by the storybook script.
First falling leaves of autumn
found you moving house,
me changing jobs
and a gap between us
which was not just
measured in miles.
When I sold the sports car,
you seemed to go with it,
the stray blonde hairs,
the lingering trace
of Kiku perfume.
All the memories
drove away with
the new owner.

Over

You were polite
when you said it was over.
You praised my charm
but told me
I wasn't right for you,
that someone else
deserved me more.
You smiled
and held my hand
when you spoke,
as if I was a small child.
You said you knew
I would understand,
and you hoped
I wasn't hurt.
It always hurts.
It's just that some smile
more than others.

Last Kiss Is Forever

You never know when
a kiss is the final kiss,
one that must last forever.
On that day in Brighton
our kiss was normal,
an everyday parting kiss
with each of us knowing
the next kiss would be soon.
Or so we thought.
But life deceived us,
swerved us off course
and tricked each of us
into thinking the other
wanted us to part.
That last kiss had to
sustain us through
too many years,
other lives, and other loves.
But no longer.
Chance has crossed
our paths again
and now our
first kiss is forever.

Lost Avenues

Once, I tried to go back,
not to find you
because you had moved,
but to see the house again.
I could still picture
driving up that narrow
tree-lined avenue
such a long time ago.
That day was warm and sunny
as it always seemed to be
on the days we met
and I can clearly see me
parking my black two-seater MG
outside the wrought iron gates
of your parents' house.
It is just one snapshot memory
from a long life of arrivals
at different houses
in different cars
for different girls.
It shows you walking to the gate
in that short lemon dress,
fair hair shining, smile wide
as a south-west sky.
I recall the tanned legs as you
dropped into the low seat
and we roared away.
Oddly, I don't remember
where we went that day,
or what we did.
I just remember my raised pulse.
Now, as I cruise the area,
much of it has changed.
Gates replaced,
extensions added,
many of the trees felled.
I can't find the right house,
nor even the right avenue.
Just like all those years ago,
when I never really found you.

Drifting

I'm floating
in a vacuum
like an astronaut
severed from his
space ship.
I'm drifting
without aim or intent,
able to survey my life
from far above,
unable to connect with it.
I can see forward and back,
see both sides of never,
and now realise why
you cut me loose.
Ninety nine per cent love
is never enough.

Dust Of Life

Doesn't matter to anyone
but the two of us
that you didn't read
the letter I sent you
so many years ago.
It's too far back to recall
just what I wrote
though I know
there would have been
a fervent declaration,
and eager promises.
Had you seen the letter,
chances are we would
still have been lost
to each other.
That time was wrong,
the dust of other lives
swirled around us,
masking the path,
erasing the hope.
Now decades later
the dust of life
has settled,
the landscape
of our existence
is sharply defined.
We see each other
with honesty and
shining truth.
It doesn't matter
when we love,
only that we do.

Friday

I wait in the cafe,
gently tapping the spoon
on the edge of
my coffee cup,
watching an android waiter
wipe the tables with
mechanical detachment.
Outside, the harsh hiss
of air-brakes startles a dog
which begins barking.
Through the window
figures glide by,
faces down,
fingers stabbing
at their smart phones.
Another Friday afternoon,
energy sapped from
the people, the city,
possibly the world.
Then you arrive,
and as you push open
the glass door,
the drabness dissolves.
Absent colours return,
the tables gleam,
the waiter smiles.
The air is cleansed,
somehow re-charged.
You always have that effect.

Lightning Kiss

We were at the top of the hill
when the storm broke,
rain slamming
from a broken sky.
There was no shelter
so we stood there
entwined,
enjoying its purity.
In just two or three minutes
we were soaked
as if thrown into a river.
Thunder cracked the air
as we clung together
and by chance
we kissed
as a lightning flash
floodlit the ground,
imprinting stark images
on the whitened landscape.
The kiss had its own tingling
electrical charge,
searing our lips,
sealing our souls.
I held you while the storm
roared around us,
the moment fused
for our eternity.

Scars

Sometimes I examine my scars,
look through the surface of my skin
to the criss-cross of cuts
that lie beneath.
Some are deep scratches,
others vicious slashes
that took a long time to heal.
A few are stab wounds
aimed at the heart
but also piercing the mind.
The pale scars were inflicted
by unnecessary razored words,
the rips and gouges by spite,
malevolence,
or worse, deceit.
They all left their marks,
some just fine faded lines
I can almost overlook
though not quite forgive.
Some still ache and hurt on dark days,
pulsing red beneath my fragile skin.
But not so often now.
As I sit quietly and watch you,
curled up on the window seat
barefoot, twisting your hair
as you read Cohen so intently,
I know that you inflicted none of them.

Postcard From The Past

Yesterday by chance,
I found a postcard
dated ten years ago.
You were in Seville
allegedly studying art.
Fly out and join me, you wrote.
It will be like old times.
You signed off with
your usual triple kisses.
I hadn't meant to keep the card,
it was inadvertently caught up
with other paperwork
and filed away.
I can picture you writing it
at some street café,
perched on the edge of the chair,
bare-legged, sun glasses,
sipping ice tea with a straw,
watching who was watching you.
It was yet another occasion
when you were between
'significant men',
as you liked to describe them,
and your cash was running low.
As usual, I got a postcard.
Nothing asked for directly,
just an invitation
and the hint of promises.
Always worked.
It did in Paris. Prague too.
And in San Francisco.
But not that time.
Not in Seville.
By then I had learned.

Border Line

I gave all my love
and took what you
said was all of yours.
But it was not.
After playing your
games for too long,
giving too many
second chances,
taking too many
emotional punches,
I have reached
the border line.
There comes a time
just like at sunset in
old Western movies,
when the hero rides away.

Left Luggage

Once we were in love.
All the signs were there,
breathless kisses,
endless calls and texts,
even limitless forgiveness
for our minor irritations.
Yet one day,
without any prelude,
disagreement
or even the need
for civilised discussion,
we became aware that
somewhere on the journey
we had put love aside
like left luggage
and moved on.
Could have happened
in that rowdy bar
when you danced with a stranger.
Maybe it was left on the train
the weekend you said
you were going to visit Julia.
It could be our love is hiding
in some dark corner,
waiting to be found again.
I don't know.
There are too many places
to search,
even if we wanted to.
Which you don't.

Messenger

You went away for a while
saying you needed
to think things over,
a bad sign and a
cruel end to a bleak,
broken day.
I sat at the window
staring out to sea
as the divide of
dark and light merged,
listening to the
spiteful drumming
of rain on the patio tiles.
Swooping suddenly
from the gloom,
a large white seagull
clattered
onto the window sill
and settled,
shaking its wings
and looking into the room
with sharp curiosity.
Its bright orange beak
tapped the glass
and its eyes had
the same cold disdain
that yours had
when you left.
The seagull was
your messenger.
I knew right then
you would never return.

Lone Witness

It is very early.
A silver sprinkle of dew
on the meadow.
Beyond, a soft cotton mist
lingers idly over
the flat, resting ocean.
I want you to see it,
be here, holding hands,
no words needed.
Just silently absorbing
the indisputable
perfection
of this new May morning.
But I am the lone witness.
You are a hundred miles away
in a place I'd best not name,
still sleeping
as one more day
of the life we don't have
slips away.

Dismissal

I knelt before you,
imploring and pleading
as if before an executioner.
Through the French windows
the deep December snow
was faintly tinged with blue.
The buckles on your high boots
twinkled in the firelight
but above, your eyes were lost
behind your fringe.
The silence told me
you had already moved on
to a new time and space.
The summary dismissal
was frosted with finality.
Wordless, you left the room.
I stayed on my knees,
clenching my fists
as if trying to hold on
to something transient.

Also by Nick Fletcher

DARK HEART
Love Poems

Reader Reviews

'Intensely private emotions polished into perfect
little works of art'
- *Eve Kerswill*

'Heartfelt, open, honest reflections of romantic love'
- *Lucy Gregory*

'Atmospherically emotional and thought provoking'
- *Sue Dyer*

'They paint beautiful images and evoke hidden memories'
- *Louise Bonner*

'Raw emotions civilised into sighs of forgiveness'
- *Helen Robertson*